Howard Hendricks has captivated audiences from coast to coast and in many parts of the world with his incisive presentation of Christian truth and a charming wit that helps make his messages unforgettable. He is professor and chairman of the Department of Christian Education, Dallas Theological Seminary, Dallas, Texas. He is a graduate of Wheaton College (A.B.) and of Dallas Seminary (Th.M. and Th.D.).

Dr. Hendricks and his wife, Jeanne, team together to speak in Family Life conferences and often share, as they do in *Heaven Help the Home* (a Victor paperback; $1.45), experiences in rearing their own family of four children—Barb, Bob, Bev, and Bill—who have either begun careers or are still in college. Dr. Hendricks is also author of *Elijah* (Moody Press; $1.00) and *Say It With Love* (Victor; $1.45), from which this book was excerpted.

contents

ISBN 0-88207-376-1

FAMILIES GO BETTER WITH LOVE

Howard G. Hendricks
with Ted Miller

Published by
VICTOR BOOKS

A division of SP Publications, Inc.

1

BEGIN WITH YOUR MATE

Hundreds of times a day a judge's gavel drops to the desk and the dismal words resound: "Divorce granted." A marriage which began with delight has ended with disillusionment. What the couple thought were stars in their eyes turned out to be sand. What began with excitement and expectation has ended with bitterness and hostility.

There's another tragedy, not as heralded but just as lamentable as a legal divorce. That is the psychological divorce: a couple who continue to live together but with minimal communication. The relationship is shattered, and for all practical purposes the marriage is dead.

The joke about the silent couple who hadn't been communicating for some time isn't far from reality: they were riding on a Sunday afternoon in the country, and he spotted two mules on the other side of the fence. For the first time in three weeks he spoke to his wife. "Some of your relatives?" he asked.

She was equal to the occasion: "Yes, on my husband's side."

And back into their stewing silence they went.

Dr. James A. Peterson, professor of sociology at the University of Southern California and a foremost authority on marriage and family life, completed an extensive study of couples who had been married between 20 and 35 years. His conclusion was that only six couples out of every hundred were satisfied and fulfilled by their marriage relationship. That makes us wonder: Why?

Face Reality

The greatest reason for failure in marriage is unrealistic expectations. The average couple enter marriage expecting a wedding to do what only God can do. It takes God to make a marriage meaningful and fulfilling. He created it. Marriage is not the product of a human pervert; it is the product of a divine plan. And God has specifications for the marriage relationship. To attempt to build a marriage without following that plan is to invite failure. That's why the psalmist said, "Except the Lord build the house, they labor in vain that build it" (Psalm 127:1).

According to my understanding of God's plan, to build a successful marriage you must develop a dynamic companionship with your partner. To focus this clearly, let's begin at the beginning. In Genesis 1, you find the repeated statement: "It was good." In verse 31, "God saw everything that He had made, and, behold, it was very good." But in chapter 2, verse 18, we see a startling contrast as He says, "It was *not good* that man should be alone." This is one of the most remarkable statements in the Scriptures. Adam had a perfect environment —no ecological problems there. He had creative genius and all of the responsibility that he could handle. He had unbroken fellowship with the infinite God. But God (not Adam) said, "It's not good that man should be alone."

Man is incomplete without the woman. No other creature

could satisfy Adam's aloneness; he had needs only a woman could supply. So God put Adam to sleep, fashioned a woman from a rib, and placed her in front of the man.

Here I'd like to improve on the King James rendering of Adam's reaction: "This is now bone of my bones" (Genesis 2:23). The Hebrew text more accurately says: "Here, now, at last!" Or as we might exclaim: "Where have you been all my life!" Adam immediately recognized Eve as the answer to his aloneness, a partner with a nature like his own to form a helping relationship.

Verse 24 states an action so fundamental in life that both Jesus Christ and the Apostle Paul later repeated it: "Therefore shall a man leave his father and his mother and shall cleave unto his wife." Reflect on the fact that God said this to Adam and Eve *before* they had any children; to two people who never had to break any family ties and therefore had no learning precedent. This is essential parental preparation. The strong human link of children to parents is thus superceded by the unique relationship of husband to wife.

Strangely, in English there are two words, *cleave,* with almost opposite meanings. As a kid in Philadelphia I used a cleaver on a pork chop and made two out of one. The "cleaving" of marriage, however, makes one out of two. The Hebrew word means "to glue, to adhere to"—a separation-proof relationship. God's ideal is one man for one woman for life, and divorce is not a live option.

I wonder when we are going to teach this to our young people. If a young couple comes into marriage thinking that divorce is a live option, the possibilities of their securing one are increased. Scripture declares that marriage is a commitment to each other for life. If we make it less, we pay the consequences.

Another component of the ideal marriage cited in Genesis 2:24 is that the couple shall be—or, become—one flesh. The Hebrew text makes clear that this is only begun, not completed, at the time of marriage. This is a process which continues as long as life continues, the cultivating of a one-flesh relationship.

All of my counseling in marriage and family problems can be categorized on the basis of these three situations: failure to truly leave the parents; failure to cleave to the one partner; or failure to develop a unified relationship. The last involves much more than the sexual relationship. A good sexual relationship does not insure a good marriage; rather, a good marriage insures a meaningful sexual relationship. Intimacy, openness, and honesty are qualities that add depth and excitement to the one-flesh relationship as years go by.

The secret of my own life and ministry is the one flesh relationship with my wife which God brought into being and is nurturing. It is my greatest satisfaction in life, and it's all of Him. I have no other explanation for it.

Work At It

Is your wife—or husband—your best friend? It's amazing how we sometimes reserve the worst for the one we love the most. I had a businessman in my office who was having problems with his marriage. I said, "What do you do for a living?"

"Oh, I sell insurance—I'm a million-dollar man."

I asked, "How do you sell your insurance?"

"Mostly over coffee or at luncheons. That's the place to sell."

"When is the last time you took out your most important client?"

"What do you mean?"

"Your wife . . . the last time you took her out as a special appointment?"

If I had hit him on the head with a two-by-four, I wouldn't have jarred him more. He said to me later, "It was just like someone pulling a curtain back. Here I spend all my life giving attention to people and I never see my wife in the same perspective!"

Some parents have the opposite problem. I'm very concerned that many young couples are spending their entire lives building their marriages and home around their children. Half of our married years will be spent without children, and the highest incidence of divorce in America is in the 45-55 age group. Why? They're out of kids, and suddenly they look at each other—and discover they're strangers. They have taken no time to cultivate their own relationship, listen to each other, and develop common interests.

How can you cultivate your love life? You have to work at it: a lot of skill, a lot of heart, and a lot of Spirit control are required. To plumb the depths of a love relationship, you must forget yourself and flow into the life of the other person.

If you really want to gauge the quality of your spiritual life, check your love dimensions. Not how often you read the Bible, not how much Scripture you have memorized, but whether the people with whom you are living regard you as a lover—a person refracting the love of Christ which He sheds into your heart.

Before the marriage, the "lover" runs around to the other side of the car to open the door for his beloved. After the marriage, he growls: "What's the matter—you got a broken arm?" Before marriage, he brings flowers. Afterward: "Save them for the funeral." Before marriage, he brings delectable candy. Now: "Aw, she's to fat already." The romance has come to a screeching halt.

I counseled a couple in my office who were having a knock-down, drag-out war of words just before they came in. Everytime I would ask the wife a question, the husband would start babbling. And when I asked him a question, she'd lecture. Finally I said, "We have to get some ground rules, OK?" So we tried to do that for half an hour and got nowhere. Then I sent her out, and I said to the man, "Do you love your wife?"

He sat up in his chair as if I had insulted him. "Of course, I love my wife," he snapped.

I said, "That's wonderful to know. When's the last time you told her?"

"Do I have to *tell* her?" he groaned.

"No, you don't have to, but it might help. I suggest that when you break the news, though, you first get her into an overstuffed chair so you don't produce a coronary."

He stiffened and shot back: "Mr., 23 years ago I told that woman I loved her, and that's still in effect till I revoke it!"

That case sounded ready for legal proceedings in more ways than one. When was the last time you told your husband, or your wife, of your love—or are you too sophisticated for that?

Are you man enough to take your wife's face in your hands and say, "I thank God for the privilege of being your husband"?

Or can you as a wife say, "I'm so thankful to God that you're mine"?

What I'm saying in effect is: *Do you have a magnet in your home?* If you don't, there's always the possibility of a magnet developing outside the home. The things that draw me irresistably from all over the world back to a little house on Silverrock Drive in Dallas is the lovely woman who is my magnet. Nothing else on earth compares with the pulling power of that magnet for me.

A student came to me some time ago and said, "Prof, I love my wife too much."

"You what?"

"I love my wife too much."

"You gotta be kidding."

"No, I think I do."

So I opened my Bible to the Ephesians 5 passage where it says husbands should love their wives as Christ loved the Church. "Do you love her that much?" I asked.

"Oh, no, of course not."

"Well, friend, you had better get with it," I urged.

That, husbands, is our assignment. And it takes the supernatural grace of God. We Americans have a ridiculous idea of what masculinity is. My Bible teaches me that the most masculine person who ever walked the earth was a Man moved with compassion. He shed tears at the loss of a loved one. When He was reviled, He didn't lash back. That takes a man. The mark of Jesus Christ is the mark of tenderness. We need an army of men who are tender not only toward the Saviour but toward their wives, their children, and others.

2 UNCONDITIONAL LOVE

We're inclined to think that love should vary according to performance, and that people need to change before we can love them more. That isn't God's kind of love, and it isn't the way to change someone. If you're trying to change your partner, stop! Instead, ask God to change *you*.

A lady in our community learned to pray that way and was the instrument to lead her husband to Christ. At Thanksgiving we had a testimony time in our church, and this husband got up and said, "As most of you know, I've been an unbeliever all of my life until this year, when God so worked in the life of my wife that I capitulated to reality."

He sat down and his wife got up and said, "I have to give you the other side of the testimony. When I first went to see Mr. Hendricks, I prayed, 'Lord, *You* love my husband, and *I'll* change him.' And nothing happened. Then I came to the place where I cried out, 'God, *I'll* love him and *You* change him.' And God changed both of us!"

The Book of Ephesians tells us how to live a heavenly life

in a hell-like world. Beginning with chapter 4 we have God's orthopedic clinic: this teaches us how to walk through war-stricken territory. Verse 31 says, "Let all bitterness, and wrath, and anger, and clamor, and evil speaking, be put away from you, with all malice." Are any of these negative things in your system? Are you willing to give them up?

I know a man who just lost a child. He had been digging into the Word of God and sharing his faith with others when God in His sovereignty took the child to heaven. The father turned bitter and his spiritual life sagged. He is saying in effect to God: "I'll serve You as long as You do what I want You to do." If God approved him on the same basis, that man would be in hell, like the rest of us. I'm confident he's going to come through, and when he reemerges, he is going to be a significant witness for Christ because he's learning God's lesson of unconditional love.

Do you love unconditionally, or on a Brownie-point system? Do you try to punish your mate by withdrawing your love? That's not love—at least not love to match the infinite value of your mate.

Notice the positive side of Paul's prescription. "Be ye kind one to another, tenderhearted, forgiving one another, even as God for Christ's sake hath forgiven you" (Ephesians 4:32).

When's the last time you said to your partner: "Sweetheart, forgive me; I was acting like a child and I know it"?

3

SUPERNATURAL CHANGE

There's another aspect that is more important than all the rest. Imagine a triangle, with the top angle representing the Lord and the other angles representing the husband and the wife in their interrelationships. Your vertical relationship with God will always affect your horizontal marital relationship.

I see this pattern followed consistently: first, you are out of fellowship with the Lord; second, you try to compensate by gaining extra concessions from your mate; third, you become self-preoccupied and ask, "What am *I* getting out of this?"

How does a person break out of that ugly, home-wrecking pattern? The most permanent and productive changes in life come through the supernatural. When God works, you have proof positive that you have encountered deep reality. Take the case of a football player friend of mine:

God had opened a ministry for me with the Dallas Cowboys football team. The first time I spoke to these men one of them professed faith in Jesus Christ as his Saviour. Then I started a Bible study class for some of the players and their wives. The new Christian called me before going to summer training camp and said, "Hey, Howie, you got something I can work on?"

I said, "Yeah, man, let me give you an assignment. Why don't you dig into the Book of Ephesians? This is a book that's a little rough, but, man, it's where life's at."

He said OK, and I gave him a modern translation for the project.

The day the Cowboy team got back into town my friend was on the phone. "Howie, I've got to see you."

"Fine. Come on over." So he came over.

He said, "Boy, I really got wiped out in the Ephesians stuff. It got serious, especially back here in this last part. I'll find it." He flipped the pages and found the verse: "Husbands, love your wives as Christ loves the Church." He looked up. "Man, no way. Frankly, that's impossible."

I said, "Why?"

"Did it ever occur to you that in my profession of football, all my life has been built around me? I've been the center of attraction. It wasn't until I became a Christian that I recognized how utterly self-centered I am. I'll take on any guy or combination of guys in the 'pit'—but in my home I'm the shyest guy in America. And now the Bible tells me to love my wife as Christ loves the Church. That's going to take some doing. Have you got any suggestions?"

"Well," I said, "what does your wife do that you really appreciate?"

"Oh," he said, "all kinds of things."

"Well, name one."

"Oh, for example, she's a fantastic cook."

"The next time she makes you a good meal," I directed, "tell her how much you appreciate it." He looked as if I'd asked him to commit murder. I said, "Well, do you think God has enough grace to help you?" He kinda thought God did. "OK," I said, "let's get down on our knees and pray about it."

He poured out his heart: "O God, I'm so self-centered and

You know it's going to take a miracle for me to do this. But I guess that's what You specialize in, so I'm trusting You."

That night the little woman knocked out one of the best meals she'd ever made—candlelight, the works. But he couldn't enjoy it. When he told me about it later, he said, "I was sitting there in agony, praying for strength to talk. After the meal I got up and went around the table and grabbed my wife—and she went as white as a sheet. I guess she thought I would cripple her. I lifted her up and said, 'Wife, that was wonderful!' "

He called me recently and said, "Howie, this is the real thing."

I said, "How do you know?"

"Man, if Jesus Christ can take a selfish guy like me and teach me how to love my wife, this must be the real thing."

And it is. Or is it—with you? Are you courageous enough, or humble enough, to open yourself to this love of God for your mate?

4

GOOD FAMILIES TAKE WORK

Socrates used to say that he wondered how men who were so careful in the training of a colt could be so indifferent to the training of their own children. Certainly the Word of God does not countenance an attitude of indifference toward children.

"Children are an heritage of the Lord," we read in Psalm 127:3. In Proverbs 22:6 we find a staggering promise: "Train up a child in the way he should go: and when he is old, he will not depart from it." That promise has never been canceled nor superseded by any higher truth. Like many of God's promises, it is inseparably linked with a command. It is God's responsibility to fulfill the promise; and it is *our* responsibility to fulfill the command by His enabling grace.

In line with New Testament truth, "training up a child" involves leading him to Christ as Saviour, preferably at an early age. To expect the child to live the Christian life when he does not possess that life is to mock him. The Christian life is not a difficult life—it is an impossible life apart from Christ's leading and power. Not until the Holy Spirit takes up His residence in an individual can that person live so as to please God.

It has been my privilege through the years to lead hundreds of people to Jesus Christ as Saviour, but I have had no greater joy than leading two of my children to Christ and seeing my wife lead the other two into a personal relationship with Him. Conversely, I can think of nothing more tragic than arriving in heaven and discovering that while hundreds came to know Christ because of my ministry, my own four children were lost because of my neglect and preoccupation.

A biblical picture of this child-training process is seen in Paul's words to Timothy as rendered in *The Living Bible*. "But you must keep on believing the things you have been taught. You know they are true, for you know you can trust those of us who have taught you. You know how, when you were a small child, you were taught the Holy Scriptures; and it is these that make you wise to accept God's salvation by trusting in Christ Jesus" (2 Tim. 3:14, 15).

Paul also said, "I know how much you trust the Lord, just as your mother Eunice and your grandmother Lois do; and I feel sure you are still trusting Him as much as ever" (2 Tim. 1:5). Here is an illustration of spiritual genetics. A godly grandmother communicated to her daughter, who in turn communicated to Timothy. The mother laid a spiritual fire in the early, impressionable years, and the Spirt of God later ignited that fire as Timothy came into a saving relationship with Christ.

The verb "to train up" occurs only three other times in the Scriptures, and each time it is translated "to dedicate." It was used of Solomon's dedicating the Temple, and so it means "to set aside for spiritual purposes."

Stimulate Their Desire

This training is further explained by the root of the Hebrew verb. It was used to describe the process of the Hebrew midwife who, at the time of birth, would plunge a finger into crushed dates and olive oil and rub the substance across the roof of the mouth of the newborn infant. The child was stimulated to suck and take nourishment, and this came to be translated: "create a desire."

How hungry and thirsty are you making your children for Jesus Christ? Somebody says, "You ought to know you can lead a horse to water, but you can't make him drink." That's right, but you can feed him salt! That's what I am suggesting. Your life ought to demonstrate the reality and the day-to-day relevance of Christian faith, so that your children want it. Only as you possess that reality do you have something significant to say. The present generation is weary of words, they are screaming for reality.

We had a lovely couple in Dallas a number of years ago. He sold his business at a loss, went into vocational Christian work, and things got rather rough. There were four kids in the family. One night at family worship, Timmy, the youngest boy, said, "Daddy, do you think Jesus would mind if I asked Him for a shirt?"

"Well, no, of course not. Let's write that down in our prayer request book, Mother."

So she wrote down "shirt for Timmy" and she added "size seven." You can be sure that every day Timmy saw to it that they prayed for the shirt. After several weeks, one Saturday the mother received a telephone call from a clothier in downtown Dallas, a Christian businessman. "I've just finished my July clearance sale and knowing that you have four boys it occurred to me that you might use something we have left. Could you use some boy's shirts?"

She said, "What size?"

"Size seven."

"How many do you have?" she asked hesitantly.

He said, "Twelve."

Many of us might have taken the shirts, stuffed them in the bureau drawer, and made some casual comment to the child. Not this wise set of parents. That night, as expected, Timmy said, "Don't forget, Mommy, let's pray for the shirt."

Mommy said, "We don't have to pray for the shirt, Timmy."

"How come?"

"The Lord has answered your prayer."

"He has?"

"Right." So, as previously arranged, brother Tommy goes out and gets one shirt, brings it in, and puts it down on the table. Little Timmy's eyes are like saucers. Tommy goes out and gets another shirt and brings it in. Out—back, out—back, until he piles 12 shirts on the table, and Timmy thinks God is going into the shirt business. But you know, there is a little kid in Dallas today by the name of Timothy who believes there is a God in heaven interested enough in his needs to provide boys with shirts.

Do your kids know that? That's fantastic communication. That, by the way, is one of the dangers of living in an affluent society. Don't gripe because your income isn't what you would like it to be. Thank God, it may be the greatest blessing that ever happened to your family, especially to your children. I have spent too much time around very wealthy individuals who would give their right arms if they could get their children back.

So child training begins with the parents. And we do well to look at God's first and preeminent commandment: "Thou shalt love the Lord thy God with all thine heart, and with all thy soul, and with all thy might" (Deut. 6:5).

Are you in love with the living Lord? Do you love Him more than you did yesterday? Is He more prominent in your life than in the days after you were born of the Spirit of God into His family?

Every day I get up I have to fall in love afresh with Jesus Christ. I have to cultivate this relationship just as I have to cultivate my relationship with my wife. This does not come by accident. And unless I have this love in my heart, I will not have it in my home. That is what Moses told Israel.

"These words, which I command you, shall be in *thine heart;* and thou shalt teach them diligently unto thy children." (6: 6,7). First in *my* heart, then in my children's. And Moses said to teach *diligently*—that means to throw everything you have into the task.

After visiting a home where the family's love for each other was deeply refreshing, a friend and I walked toward my car, and he said, "Some people have the most wonderful children— some people do, some people don't." Just then I noticed a neatly manicured lawn, and I responded, "Some people have the most beautiful lawns even in August."

He looked at me and said slowly: "If you have a beautiful lawn in August in Texas, you have worked at it."

Yes, good lawns and good families take *work*.

5

UNDERSTANDING EACH OTHER

Homes are coming apart because their members are; that is, everyone moves within his separate orbit and home becomes the filling station where we check the gas and chassis for replenishment and repair, but we don't spend much time there. We are like ships passing in the night, and very little life flows from one member to another.

As a marriage and family counselor, I encounter some very interesting cases. Some time ago a boy was picked up by a police squad car, and the first thing he said to the officer was, "You aren't going to tell my old man, are you?"

He replied, "I'd be interested in hearing why you don't want your father to know."

"I'll tell you," he answered. "He's not interested in me; he's too busy."

When the policeman called the father about his son, the irate response was: "What in the world are you calling me for?"

The case was referred to me, and it was my privilege to lead the father to Jesus Christ. He became a different person, and he became concerned about his family problems.

He came to my office one day and said, "OK, now what do I do? Let's put this thing back together."

"Friend, this is going to take time," I warned him. "You can't decimate the bridges for 15 years and rebuild them overnight. What does your son like to do?"

He had to think for a long time but finally came up with, "He likes to go fishing."

I said, "OK, why don't you plan a fishing trip with him?"

He went home and in typical adult fashion announced: "Son, next week we are going fishing."

The boy looked him in the eye and said, *"You're* going fishing. I've already got some things planned."

The father blew his top. He gave the boy a portion of his mind he couldn't really afford to lose, and the son countered very calmly: "A number of years ago I wanted to go fishing, and you were too busy. Now you want to go fishing, and I'm too busy. What's your problem?"

The father came back to my office like a whipped dog to find out what he could do. He was so low he began to realize he must trust God to do what he himself could not. He could appreciate the fact that his family needed to *understand* each other, not just talk at each other.

Sometimes I encounter a family where communications are so frozen that I get them all in my office and we start a conversation. I only allow one person to talk at a time, and after one expresses himself, I ask another member: "Now tell me what you heard him say." And we stick to that until everyone in the group can say back to the satisfaction of the speaker what he said. It's painful and time consuming, but it's amazing how for the first time they begin to hear what the individual is really saying. Then they have the possibility of communicating.

Some parents thoroughly involve their children in the father's work. I was in the home of a Chicago executive and had wonderful fellowship with the whole family. In the kitchen I saw the walls plastered with the advertising of the executive's company and I said, "Well, you do have a promotional program here."

"No," he replied, "that's my ministry. We pray for that as a family."

That's vastly different from the family that speaks of the factory or the office or what-have-you as the "monster" that is supposedly ruining their lives.

6 | ENJOY LIFE TOGETHER

In Deuteronomy 6:7 there are two key terms which spell out the nature of parental education. One is *teach* (that's formal, structured). The other is *talk* (that's informal, situational). A good parent uses both kinds of instruction, realizing that informal times together are actually teaching situations, for good or ill.

Do you take the time and make the effort to have fun in your home? Do your kids enjoy their home? To me, the poorest representative of Jesus Christ is the Christian who doesn't know what it is to enjoy life. Many of us are so glum we look as if we're on the road to hell instead of the road to heaven. The only people in the world today who are in a position to laugh and rejoice are those who are secure in Jesus Christ!

I can remember in the early days of my family recreation we started out with a tent. My wife was not exactly the tenting type, but it's amazing what you can get used to. Now that my children are pretty well grown, it is interesting to ask what they remember most. The two boys remember when they and I stayed in a pup tent—talk about togetherness, it was wall-to-wall!

Before we went to bed that night, I looked to the west and said, "Hey, fellows, you'd better dig those trenches deep around the edge; it looks like we may get some rain." Well, we got nine inches of rain in four hours. And we ended up two miles down the creek drying ourselves out under a shelter and talking about the Lord and His protective hand. Back in Dallas, we found out later, 13 people died that night from the storm. You know, that lesson in God's protection wasn't sermon number 293 in my file; that was real life, and it communicated!

One of the great fun times in our home has been the Friday night "Hendricks Talent Theater." We would put old clothes and junk in a bag and drag them out for an unrehearsed drama. Television was boring beside our production. I came out of those experiences with my ribs sore from laughing. Have you ever examined the atmosphere of your home and asked how attractive it is? You say, "I'm so glad you asked; we just finished decorating it. Man, we've got wall-to-wall carpeting, coordinating drapes."

No, I didn't ask you that—that's your junk. I asked you, how attractive is your home? I go into many Christian homes today and frankly I am repelled. They are covered over with legalism. There is what I call a suffocating fog of moralism, and every time the kid moves we're nailing him to the floor. Every time he turns around we're cramming something down his throat. "All right, let's get together; we're going to have Bible study now." Not too long ago, one dear lady blew her cork in the midst of the family worship. She shouted at the kids, "Shut up; you ought to hear what God has to say!" Some of us say shut up so many times, our children are like the kid who was eight years old before he discovered has name was not Shut Up. What are you like to live with?

We had two students at the seminary from a home in California that has sent all its children into Christian work. Sometime ago I was with one of them and I asked: "What do you remember most about your father?"

He thought for a minute and then said, "Two things stand out in my mind, and they're quite contrasting. The first thing is getting up early in the morning for a paper route and seeing my father on his knees praying. That made a profound impression on me. The second thing is his rolling on the floor with laughter with us kids!" What a combination—on the floor in prayer and on the floor in laughter! By the way—what will your children remember you for?

Live Honestly Before Children

The atmosphere of the home inculcates Christian truth more effectively than the words we speak. The attitude of truthfulness, for example, is more caught than taught. A student asked me sometime ago what I thought was the most important trait for my children to gain. I told him I'd have to think about that a while, and I came to the conclusion that if I had to choose only one characteristic for my children it would be honesty. I want children who are honest to God, to other people, and honest with themselves. And I realized it is most likely to be conveyed through example.

The phone rings. It's for Tom. Tom's wife, Mary, asks, with her hand securely covering the mouthpiece, "Tom, are you here?"

Tom deceitfully replies, "No, I'm not here!"

Now, you can tell your child all you want about honesty, but you are teaching him to be a first-class liar.

I find that young people from Christian homes are rebelling most over phoniness and lack of reality, not from having parents who are not perfect. I find that the parent who is honest enough to admit "Buddy, I goofed; I apologize" comes over like horse radish.

Let's suppose that I were to tell you I sell the best hair restorer lotion in existence—it's guaranteed. You take another look at my bald head and go into hysterics. Should I blame you? But this is what is happening in many Christian homes. Parents are trying to teach truth and love for God when they don't possess them. If the reality of Jesus Christ has not gripped you, you cannot pass it on to your children. I sometimes think we might communicate Christ better to our children if we were deaf and dumb because we would realize how much we need Jesus Christ helping us.

I have trouble with this, too. I can understand that I need the control of the Holy Spirit to address a crowd, or to witness, or to teach a Bible class. But who needs the control of the Spirit for playing a game with the kids? Paul says, "Whatsoever you do in word or in deed, do all in the name of the Lord Jesus" (Col. 3:17). There's only one way we can do that, and that's under the Spirit's control.

When I had the privilege of speaking to 8,000 people at a Sunday School convention in California my students told me they'd be praying for me. I felt it, and the good results were obviously from God. Then I caught a plane back to Dallas. After my wife welcomed me back, she got down to reality and said, "Honey, I've got bad news for you. The sewer has broken."

Did you call the repairman?

"Four times. He says it's caved in."

"Well, let's get it fixed."

"He said it will cost $425 to dig a trench out to the alley."

"Not $425! I'll dig it myself."

So I enlisted my son—he's a physical fitness buff—and we went to work. If you've ever dug in Texas gumbo, you know it's like concrete. We got out six or eight feet and discovered the pipe was going in a downward direction! We dug in again, and finally we came to the break—sure enough, it was caved in. We stood there in the trench meditating and suddenly someone flushed the toilet!

Was the Holy Spirit with me in that soggy trench—as He had been when I was speaking to 8,000 people about Christian truth? If not, I don't have much to talk about. If the Holy Spirit doesn't control your temper at the office or your tongue when you're around godless people, then we shouldn't talk about having the fullness of the Spirit. He has to work in the nitty-gritty of life, or He isn't working in us.

Some of my toughest tests come at home—after God has used me in a public ministry to other people. And the more you try to live distinctly for Jesus Christ, the more you will understand what reality is—because you'll face the basic issues and find you can't handle them except in Jesus' power.

"Whom the Lord loves, He chastens." Is God disciplining you? He loves you, and He has saved you so you may be conformed to the image of His Son. We remember that even Jesus learned obedience by the things that He suffered. Your children have a great need for adequate models—are you one? Neither am I—that's why the Lord is working on us.

7

EXPRESS LOVE FOR YOUR CHILDREN

Another thing we parents can work on is expressing our love for one another. I hope you're not ashamed to express your love in front of your children. The best thing a father can do for his son is to love his son's mother; the best thing a mother can do for her daughter is to love her daughter's father. In this context the children learn to give and receive love for each other. And you'll never develop a pervert in this kind of environment.

Maybe you get all shook up over your kids fighting. My counsel as a veteran referee is: don't sweat it. Our two girls and two boys had some knock-down, drag-out skirmishes—the Civil War all over again. They are now in their teens and twenties, and I dare anyone to scowl at my daughter when her brother is around. They are so close that tears roll down their faces when they greet one another at an airport, and they couldn't care less what others think of their affection.

How do you develop love? It comes over a period of time and as a product of a pattern. We can do a lot of things to encourage the expression of love.

Birthdays have always been significant in our home. I remember when my girls were learning to cook, and the younger one decided she would make doughnuts for Bob's birthday. They turned out like rocks; every time you'd swallow a bite you could hear the splash. But Bob ate the last one of those doughnuts, hugged his sister, and said, "Man, what a cook you are, Bev."

Recently I had a thrilling experience in an unexpected place. I was in an opulent home—probably in the $500,000 class. It belongs to a man who told me: "I ended up at the top of my field but at the bottom of life." Then he found Jesus Christ as his Saviour, and he and his wife began studying the Word to find out how the Lord wanted them to train their children.

I went into their gorgeous living room and almost got lost in the living room rug—felt like I might get a severe case of mink rash on the spot. Interior decorators have convinced us that a living room has to have a center of interest, but right in the center of that lovely room was a peanut butter jar holding wilted daisies. I found out that her son had picked them for her on his way home from school, and I said, "I bet they have a lot of meaning to you."

She beamed and said, "That's the most wonderful thing in this room."

My wife taught me that a relationship is far more important than a clean home. We can have a *Better Homes and Gardens* layout and a *Mad* family life. The floor can be quickly cleaned after little feet have muddied it, but bruised relationships are not so easily restored.

Occasionally I have had the assignment of going into an exclusive home in Dallas and telling the parents that the court has decided to put away their child permanently. When these people have no internal resources, they come unglued at the seams. We had one boy in custody who drove the most expensive brand sports car in America and had a monthly allowance of $475. He had just about everything except parents who gave of themselves. The stuff you buy will never substitute for you; there is no substitute for a personal, loving relationship in the family.

You know what I have to do? People call me on the phone. "Prof, will you come over and preach to us?"

"No, I'm awfully sorry, I won't."

"You won't? How come?"

Well, I've learned to say, "I'm otherwise engaged," which, .being interpreted, means, "I'm going to stay home."

A few years ago I used to be a little more direct. Somebody would call and ask me to speak on a certain night.

"No, I'm awfully sorry, I can't come that night. I'm going to stay home and play with my kids."

"You what?"

"I'm going to stay home and play with my kids."

"You mean you're not coming to preach to us?"

"No, I'm not coming to preach to you."

Somebody says, "Oh, that's how liberalism gets started in the seminary." And if I listen to that kind of garbage I could lose my whole family in the process. We must not allow anybody to control our lives except the Spirit of God, and there is no conflict between duty and Christian experience. Your call to be a parent is not in conflict with your call to be a Christian. If it is, you should have remained a celibate!

I don't know what my kids will remember me for. I hope they will be able to remember me as a father who loved them and enjoyed them. I believe the greatest challenge confronting Christian fathers today is to become articulate concerning our faith so we can communicate it to our children. Our homes should be laboratories for instructing our children formally and informally. Homes should be training grounds for developing habit patterns that serve Jesus Christ. And then we'll avoid the tragedy described in Judges 2:10—a generation arose which knew not the Lord.